Growing Up Pagan
A Workbook for Wiccan Families

Raine Hill
with Drawings by Gillian M. Pearce

Schiffer
Publishing Ltd

4880 Lower Valley Road Atglen, PA 17566

Dedication

To my wonderful husband, Cal. Thank you for your unconditional love and for sharing your life with me. I don't know what I did in a past life to deserve you, but I'm glad I did it. I love you more.
Also to my father, Thomas Martin. I miss you.

Cover Photo:
United Kids©Dawn Hudson. Pentagramm©Thomas Durst. Images from BigStockPhoto.com

Copyright © 2009 by Raine Hill
Library of Congress Control Number: 2008938539

Designed by John Cheek
Cover design by Bruce Waters
Type set in Burton's Nightmare 2000/NewBskvll BT

ISBN: 978-0-7643-3143-5

Printed in China

The following images from BigStockPhoto.com. Antique Replica Jewelery Box © Nicolaaas Traut, Artistic Blue Spiral © Todd Arena, Bark © SeaWaters, Blank Chalkboard © Carolina-Smith, Pencil Top Erasers © James Duplass, Pencils © Elena Elisseeva, Pile of Books © Jostein Hauge, School Supplies on white background w path © Michale Flippo, Clock-Calendar © Konstantin Remizov, Hot Summer Sun © Petr Vaclavek, Id Moon © Aravind Teki, iron cauldron on white © James Steidl, Mouse © Marion Wear, Night Day © Eray Haciosmanoglu, Rabbit Running © cheng en lim, Sand © keith brooks, Sea View © JinYoung Lee, Silent Night, Moonlit Night © Ioana Drutu, Snowy Owl Swooping Down © Linda Bucklin, Sunny Flower © Cindy Haggerty, turtle © Alessandro Bolis, Weaved Reed Texture © Natalia Shmeliova, Witch Broomstick © Olga Pshenichka.

Schiffer Books are available at special discounts for bulk purchases for sales promotions or premiums. Special editions, including personalized covers, corporate imprints, and excerpts can be created in large quantities for special needs. For more information contact the publisher:

Published by Schiffer Publishing Ltd.
4880 Lower Valley Road
Atglen, PA 19310
Phone: (610) 593-1777; Fax: (610) 593-2002
E-mail: Info@schifferbooks.com

Please visit our web site catalog at www.schifferbooks.com

We are always looking for people to write books on new and related subjects. If you have an idea for a book, please contact us at the above address.

This book may be purchased from the publisher.
Include $5.00 for shipping.
Please try your bookstore first.
You may write for a free catalog.

In Europe, Schiffer books are distributed by:
Bushwood Books
6 Marksbury Ave.
Kew Gardens
Surrey TW9 4JF
England
Phone: 44 (0)208 392-8585
Fax: 44 (0)208 392-9876
E-mail: Info@bushwoodbooks.co.uk

Website: www.bushwoodbooks.co.uk
Free postage in the UK. Europe: air mail at cost.
Try your bookstore first.

6 Marksbury Ave.
Kew Gardens
Surrey TW9 4JF England
Phone: 44 (0) 20 8392-8585; Fax: 44 (0) 20 8392-9876
E-mail: info@bushwoodbooks.co.uk
Website: www.bushwoodbooks.co.uk
Free postage in the U.K., Europe; air mail at cost.

Author Note

Thank you for purchasing "Growing Up Pagan: A Workbook for Wiccan Families." As many of you know, the term "Pagan" encompasses people of many different traditions: Druids, Asatru, Wiccans, Witches, and many others. This book focuses on some of the very basic teachings of Wicca. Since ideas surrounding Wicca are so diverse, I feel that I should add this "disclaimer." I know that each tradition within Wicca (maybe even within each person in the same tradition!) sees and explains things differently, so please note that the contents of this book are but one perspective surrounding the basics of Wiccan beliefs and are meant to enhance your own teachings.

Knowing that this path is a lifelong study, I have studied long and hard, as most of us do. Still, please know that I am in no way saying that my beliefs are the one true way; I am simply hoping to ensure that children of Pagan homes have access to basic material about their religion just as children of other faiths have had for generations.

If you are reading this, you are probably residing in the Northern Hemisphere. For that reason, the Sabbats (Wheel of the Year) will be described from the perspective of someone living in the Northern Hemisphere. (The actual dates of Sabbats are affected depending upon where in the world you live.) Also, for the purposes of this book, I do use the terms "Witch" and "Wiccan" interchangeably; not all will agree with this. However, I believe our diversity and open-minded thoughts are what keeps Paganism and Wicca rich and alive.

Mythology has been handed down through oral stories as well as written and rewritten tales. For instance, the Celts had no written word, so they told stories verbally to help teach lessons and explain the world around them. Pagans have used these myths as a basis for their beliefs for many generations. The myths that I have rewritten have been adapted into "story form" to be more appealing to a younger audience. My goal, through these stories, explanations, and games, are designed to reinforce what the stories teach, and to help children growing up in a Pagan (specifically Wiccan) household to learn the mythology and customs behind their religion. As there are many myths related to Wicca, these stories are, of course, one viewpoint. I hope that you and the child(ren) for which this guide is intended enjoy this work as much as I have enjoyed writing it.

In love and light,
Raine Hill

The Moon as a Symbol of the Goddess

Wicca is known as an "Earth religion." This means that we see and feel the God and Goddess in everything in nature. Trees, plants, stars, the moon and sun all hold a special place in the heart of a Witch. We see the moon as a symbol of the Goddess and so we celebrate the phases of the moon. When the moon is full, we have what is known as an esbat celebration. This is a full moon ritual, when we give thanks to the Goddess for all that She has given us.

When the moon is building its way up to full, it is known to be "waxing," as it appears to get larger and brighter. After the night of the full moon, it begins to "wane" or appear to get smaller in the sky. You may already have seen a symbol that stands for the waxing, full, and waning moon phases. Some Wiccans also use the symbol to stand for the Goddess in Her three aspects of Maiden, Mother, and Crone. The symbol for the Triple Goddess and the Moon Phases is on the next page.

Triple Goddess/Moon Phases

Practice Drawing Triple Goddess Moon Phases Symbol Below:

The Sun as a Symbol of the God

The sun is seen by Wiccans as a symbol of the God. He is thought of as being responsible for the growing of crops. The sun is very important for this. Much of Wiccan belief is adapted from the practices of ancient people who thought there were different Gods and Goddesses for almost every event in their lives. For instance, some believed there was a God whom they called Cernunnos (ker-NOO-nos) who was in charge of a successful hunt. The ancient people really needed a good hunting season in order to eat all winter, so they prayed heavily to the God Cernunnos to help them. Since the stag that they hunted had horns, they imagined Cernunnos as The Horned God, with deer-like antlers on his head. Before a large hunt, the ancient peoples would perform a ritual known as "sympathetic magick" where they would wear the horns and skins of animals and pretend to spear each other. They believed that, by doing this, they would have a successful hunt and be able to eat throughout the bitter cold winter when food does not grow. Later, Cernunnos became known by the shorter names of Cerne and Herne. Many Pagans still worship this ancient Celtic God. On the next page is a symbol that many Witches use for the Horned God.

Horned God Symbol

Practice Drawing the Horned God Symbol Below:

The Wiccan Rede

Some Pagans believe this was written around 1910 by Adriana Porter; others credit Wiccan author Doreen Valiente. No matter who wrote it, it is a wonderful rede to live by. Memorize this and practice it often, as it is very important to Pagans and Wiccans.

The Wiccan Rede

Bide the Wiccan law ye must

In perfect love and perfect trust.

Eight words the Wiccan Rede fulfill:

'An ye harm none, do as ye will.

What you put forth will come back to thee

So ever mind the Law of Three.

Follow this in mind and heart,

Merry ye meet and merry ye part.

Please note that there is a very long version of this piece, credited to a woman named Doreen Valiente. This is the mid-length version that I learned as a younger Witch. The very short version is this: 'An ye harm none, do as ye will.)

The First Battle of the Gods and the Giants
A Creation Story

Long, long ago, before there were humans on the Earth, there was only the Goddess Dana. She lived by the sea and sat under Her Rowan tree each day and talked to the waves as they rolled in. After a time, She became very lonely and longed for someone to talk to. One day, She decided to build a son and a daughter from the sand on the beach and some of the bark from the Rowan tree. Dana then took a cup of water from the sea and blessed it with the gift of life. She then sprinkled the son and daughter with the holy water, saying these words as she worked:

> Sands of the beach,
> Bark of the tree
> Give life to each,
> Making children for me.

Upon hearing these words, they were not sand anymore, but living beings. The Goddess Dana breathed Her life into them, making them Gods and Goddesses who could talk with Her and keep Her company. Dana then threw the remaining bark from the Rowan tree into the sea. Upon falling into the sea water, the bark turned into many giants who continued to live in the sea. Dana and her son and daughter lived happily on the beach and became very close.

Dana's son decided the Earth needed animals as well; so He made deer, dogs, snakes, and every other animal from the bark of the same Rowan tree. The animals gathered around Him and became his companions and the God watched over the animals. He loved the animals very much, but He was particularly fond of the stag (a type of deer). He even gave himself the horns of a stag and frolicked with them every day. He named himself "Cernunnos" which means "Horned One."

Dana's daughter was a wonderful shapeshifter, meaning that She could change Herself into any animal that She chose. After becoming many different animals, she found that Her favorite was the crow. Each day, She would shapeshift into a crow and fly over the sea to entertain herself. Since she could shapeshift, she named herself "Morrigan," which means "Phantom Queen."

After a time, the giants of the sea got very jealous of the God and Goddesses. The giants decided that they would send great waves to the Earth to try to drown Dana, Cernunnos, Morrigan and all the animals. One day, as Morrigan was flying over the sea as a crow, she overheard the plot of the giants and warned Cernunnos and Dana. Since Dana was the Mother Goddess, she felt she needed to protect Her children. From the sands of the beach, She crafted several people to help with battle against the giants of the sea; but the newly-made people were not Gods and Goddesses, simply humans.

To prepare for battle, Morrigan took a sharp shell from the beach and split herself into three different Goddesses: Badb, Macha, and The Morrigan, all fierce Goddesses of war. Macha made Herself a horse-drawn chariot to use in battle, while Badb had a magick cauldron in which She could see the future. The Morrigan cut Herself a wooden spear and a breast plate from a nearby birch tree for protection in war.

Cernunnos gathered His animals and told them of the upcoming fight with the giants of the sea. He taught them to be fierce when threatened and ready to attack when needed. The stag gathered around Cernunnos and lowered their heads, showing their sharp horns and preparing for battle. The wild dogs gathered in packs, growling and baring their strong teeth. The snakes hissed and showed their fangs; they were ready to protect the Gods and Goddesses and strike at the giants when they came ashore.

Each day, Badb was studying the water in Her magick cauldron to see what the giants were up to. One day, She was peering into Her cauldron and She could see the giants rising from the waters of the sea, causing great waves to form as they headed towards the shore. Immediately, Badb told everyone what was happening and they set themselves into action. Like the fiercest warriors ever known, the Gods and Goddesses and all the animals headed to the shore to meet the angry giants of the sea. The giants had caused huge waves to come upon the Earth. This frightened the humans so badly that they retreated far into the forest for protection in the tall trees, leaving the fighting to the more capable God and Goddesses and the loyal animals of the Earth.

Macha was not the least bit afraid and jumped onto Her chariot, Her long black hair blowing wildly in the breeze from the large waves. The horses snorted loudly and nodded their heads, knowing the war had begun. Macha raised Her whip to the air, threw Her head back and screamed louder than the crashing of the waves:

> Lightning of the sky, waves of the sea:
> Come to my aid; you must help me!
> Lightning strike them in their tracks;
> Waves rush in and knock them back!
> Evil giants shall not win;
> Lightning, waves, let the battle begin!

The second Macha screamed these words, the lightning crashed from the sky and struck several dozen giants, killing them instantly. The huge waves knocked over many giants climbing from the sea and drowned them. Macha charged towards the giants, driving Her chariot straight through them, killing several hundred.

The battling Dana raised her fist into the air and screamed a battle cry so loud that it split the sky:

Clouds of white, sky of blue
Open the skies and let the Gods through!
Your help We need; your help, please give—
Defeat the giants so we may live!

Upon hearing Dana's cries, the heavens split open and small pieces of the sky fell to the sea. From these small pieces, new Gods and Goddesses were formed to help fight in the long battle. The sea churned with fury; the battling Gods, Goddesses, and giants fought bitterly in the deep waters. The Morrigan then threw Her magick spear and it killed dozens in one instant. Cernunnos commanded his animals to attack the giants.

Many of the giants became very afraid and hurried back into the water where they were killed by the Gods and Goddesses of the sea. All the Gods and Goddesses of the Earth, Sky, and Sea did their jobs to defeat the giants. When the giants were so afraid that they finally retreated deep into the water, the waves died down and the battle was over. The humans came down from the trees and started the human race, having many children and populating the Earth. A few of the giants had sneaked past the battle and ran far, far, far from the sea, making their homes on land. They started their own race, called the Fomorians, who vowed that they would one day take over the world from the Gods and Goddesses. This was but the first of many battles that took place later.

13

The First Battle of the Gods and the Giants
A Creation Story

© Raine Hill

ACROSS

1 Morrigan loved to shapeshift into this animal

5 Her name means "Phantom Queen"

7 The Mother Goddess; mother of Cernnunos, Morrigan and others

8 Cernunnos was particularly fond of this animal

9 Where the giants lived, before the battle

DOWN

1 This name means "Horned One"

2 The Morrigan fought with this

3 After making their home on land, the giants called their race
_____

4 An aspect of The Morrigan who had a chariot

6 She peered into Her cauldron to watch the giants

Solution on page 57

The First Battle of the Gods and the Giants

Find the words in the grid. Words can go horizontally, vertically and diagonally in all eight directions.

```
L C E R N U N N O S D
S N A I R O M O F A L
C C C S C W G S N N S
V N R N E H T A A N P
S Z O Y K A A G G E E
K T W R G M I R L L A
A B N L Q R N T I M R
H B Q A R D T M W O F
C D Y O I A V G B R T
A A M W B G C Q L B K
M B L I G H T N I N G
```

Badb	giants
battle	lightning
Cernunnos	Macha
chariot	Morrigan
crow	sea
Dana	spear
Fomorians	stag

Solution on page 58

The Myth of Pandora's Box

Pandora, whose name means "All Gifted," was the most beautiful woman ever created. Zeus, the most powerful of the Roman gods, had ordered the other gods and goddesses to give Pandora a gift from each of them. First the goddesses each gave Pandora a gift; then Apollo and Zeus:

Aphrodite gave to Pandora the qualities of beauty and personality;

Demeter showed her how to grow herbs and corn;

Athena taught her to spin the most beautiful cloth anyone had ever seen.

The god Apollo taught her to sing more beautifully than anyone else ever had.

Zeus, on the other hand, gave Pandora the quality of being curious. As a final gift, he then gave her a stunningly beautiful golden box, which he told her she should never open.

Epimetheus, with whom Zeus was very angry, would be the chosen husband for Pandora. When Zeus brought Pandora before Epimetheus, he was so taken by her beauty and fine-spun clothing that he forgot all about his feud with Zeus and accepted his wife instantly. They had a wonderful life together with Pandora tending her garden, spinning fantastic cloths, and singing beautifully all the while. All the gifts that had been given to Pandora seemed to make her the most perfect woman to be Epimetheus' wife—except her curiosity. Each day she would pass by Zeus' gift, the beautiful golden box, and touch it lightly. She so wanted to know what was inside! In her most lovely singing voice, she would sing her melodic song:

Oh, beautiful box that shines so bright
What magickal wonders you hold inside.
I wish I may, I wish I might
Know all the secrets that you hide.

Surely, if the outside of the box was so beautiful, shiny and inviting, what it held must certainly be wonderful! Still, Pandora would simply polish the box with her dust cloth and walk away—after all, she had been forbidden to open it.

One day, her curiosity almost overwhelming her, she decided she should hide the box so she wouldn't think about it and be tempted. Oh, Pandora tried! She hid it in the dark cellar of her beautiful home she shared with her husband, Epimetheus. For a hundred years, the box sat untouched. Then one day, Pandora was doing some spring cleaning and happened upon the box again. She dusted it off and was again dumbfounded by its sparkling beauty. She thought a tiny peek wouldn't hurt, so she opened the box just a tad. Instantly, out flew dark winged demons that screeched so loudly that Pandora dropped the box to cover her ears! Out came every nasty, ugly, bad quality of the world: Death, Hunger, Greed, Hate, Jealousy, and a thousand others behind them.

Pandora was so frightened, she ran from the cellar while all the demons flew out of her house and out into the world. She never got to see who was the last to exit the beautiful golden box. Slowly, carefully, and with shining determination, the final one in Pandora's box arose and spoke to all who would listen:

I am Hope, to whom you must call.
I will enter your heart, making sure you don't fall.
When other things start to get you down
Know, in your heart, I'm always around.

To this day, with all the horrible things that we humans are up against in the world, we hold onto Hope, for she is the most powerful of everything in Pandora's box. Hope can always be invited into our hearts and help us overcome if only we remember her.

*** This myth should be easy to understand. Always hold Hope in your heart to help us through the difficult times. ***

Pandora's Box Crossword

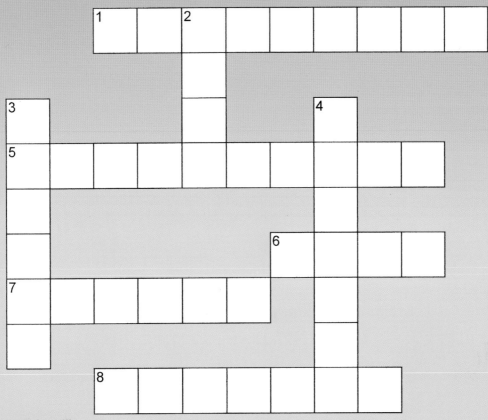

(c) Raine Hill

ACROSS

1 Gave Pandora the gift of beauty
5 Pandora's husband
6 Gave Pandora the beautiful golden box
7 Taught Pandora to sing beautifully
8 This name means "All Gifted"

DOWN

2 Last to leave the magick box
3 Where Pandora hid the beautiful golden box
4 Showed Pandora how to grow corn

Solution on page 58

The Myth of Pandora's Box

Find the words in the grid. Words can go horizontally, vertically and diagonally in all eight directions.

```
S  U  E  H  T  E  M  I  P  E  B  M
Z  L  V  N  Q  H  K  X  E  N  Y  A
C  E  L  C  K  R  K  G  H  X  P  R
U  X  U  T  Z  K  A  Z  O  Z  C  O
R  F  O  S  Q  I  J  B  K  M  L  D
I  Q  F  L  R  L  N  K  L  K  G  N
O  W  K  R  L  E  L  M  C  T  K  A
S  C  A  X  D  O  M  Q  H  S  T  P
I  M  K  L  H  P  O  B  D  B  J
T  L  O  Y  Z  N  P  A  F  O  R  N
Y  G  D  E  M  E  T  E  R  G  V  W
G  W  E  D  D  I  N  G  G  I  F  T
```

Apollo
curiosity
Demeter
Epimetheus
gods
golden box
Hope
marriage
Pandora
wedding gift
Zeus

Solution on page 59

How to Make a "My First Altar"

A Wiccan altar is made to remind you of the love of the God and Goddess and the Elements of the Earth. The love of the Lord and Lady are with you every day and night as they offer their love and support in your life. The four Elements of the Earth are also powerful forces that influence our lives every day. The Elements of the Earth are: Earth, Air, Fire, and Water and each one has its own influences and magickal properties.

You should set up your altar in your bedroom (or other quiet area that your parents approve) so that you can see it often and be reminded of the beauty of nature and the love of the Gods.

You can make your altar from almost anything—a small table or even a new wooden kitchen cutting board have been used in my home as altars. I like to use a square table or area because I can then mark the quarters more easily: North at the top of the square, South at the bottom, East on the right, and West on the left.

Before making your altar, I would suggest going on a nature walk to look for things to put on your new altar. Go out in your own yard, or take a longer walk with your family. Use whatever items seem to call to you. You will end up with an altar that is special to you and only you.

North

Since the North, for many Wiccans, stands for the element of Earth, you could find something that is of the Earth: a rock, a leaf, a pinecone, even a crystal if you have one. You could then put this item at the top of your altar to mark North. The color for the North is usually thought of as Green, so you could use something green if you like.

East

For the East, Wiccans usually think of the element of Air. To remember Air, you could place a feather or a piece of unlit incense on the right side of your altar space. Incense is attributed to the Element of Air because its smoke is thought to carry our prayers to the Gods. The Quarter Color for East is usually thought of as yellow; think about this in making your decision, if you like.

South

Moving on to the South (at the bottom of your altar), you could put something that reminds you of fire. What reminds you of the Element of Fire? A match or an unlit candle would be only two of the many good choices. Since the Quarter Color of the South is red in most traditions, a red candle might be nice. (Leave the candles unlit. Do not light the candle unless your parents are with you, since this could be dangerous!)

West

The last Quarter would be on the left of your altar: the West and its correspondent, the Element of Water. To mark the West, you could put a little water in a small dish or cup and place it in this area of your altar space. You could also use a shell that you find at the beach. The color for the West is usually thought of as blue. We often think of water as being blue, such as the deep, blue sea.

Figures

If you like, you could fashion figures of the God and Goddess, however you may see them, from modeling clay. Let them dry thoroughly, then put them in the middle of the altar, between all the symbols of the elements.

Pentacle

You can also color the pentacle (found on another page of this book), cut it out, and put it on the middle of your altar, under your images of the Goddess and God.

Now your altar is all set up! Each time you walk by your new altar, you can be reminded of the four Elements of the Earth and of the love of the God and Goddess. Of course, this is only one idea to get you started; there are many ways you can make it. It is all up to you!

Now that you have an altar of your own, you can learn some prayers to thank the God and Goddess for all you have been given in your life. You can even make up your own chants or prayers so that they are special to you. Here are two daily blessings: one for after waking up and one to say before bedtime. It is always nice to have your altar in sight, but you could just think about the God and Goddess and They will be with you.

These blessings are fairly short, so if you say them every morning and night, you will learn them before you know it!

The Four Quarters

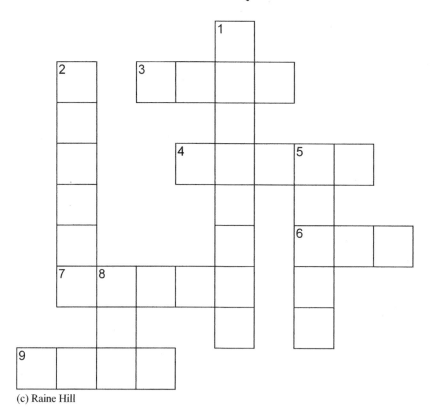

(c) Raine Hill

ACROSS

3 Color of the Direction of West
4 The Quarter Color of the North
6 The Color of the Direction of South
7 The Element of the West
9 The Element of the South

DOWN

1 The Four Directions are also called _____.
2 The color of the Direction of East
5 The Element of the North
8 The Element of the East

Solution on page 59

Morning Blessing

Powerful Lord and Lady
of the moon, stars, and sun
Shower me in your blessings
as the new day has begun.

Nighttime Blessing

The day is done
the night is here.
Bless me tonight
and all I hold dear.
Allow me to wake
to a brand new day
Filled with love
in every way.

Morning Blessing

Find the words in the grid. Words can go horizontally, vertically and diagonally in all eight directions. The lines of this poem are not in order.

```
I N Y O U R B L E S S I N G S
X N K J Y F M M V N N Y K C Q
O N L L T H M M Q U R K V T N
F T M O F L B T G L M N P R Y
T M N K R Q T E R V W O R P A
H B C U M D B D T Z W N N T D
E L H T S S A G K E C B L X W
M X N W A D M N R L M J J M E
O Y N H G X N F D W H V F N N
O Z K X L W U A Q L Q V H M E
N T C T G L L Q S J A M J Y H
C H R R R B K R Q R T D L Z T
K B C G K M B T N M A W Y Q S
E M R E W O H S B H T T J Q A
K B T R R K V Z M B H Q S G Q
```

as the new day
has begun
in Your blessings
Lord and Lady
of the moon
Powerful
Shower me
stars and sun

Solution on page 60

Nighttime Blessing

Find the words in the grid. Words can go horizontally, vertically and diagonally in all eight directions. The lines of this poem are not in order

```
N T N W A X P E N T M Z H K F
K T N N N J L V B H B T H E G
P O G M D B T O L E M H L K N
P A C L A R B L E D I E D A J
M B F W L B F H S A N N L W D
C R R C L V L T S Y E I J O V
V A R X I R B I M I V G J T N
Z N K D H F K W E S E H V E T
M D M R O M C D T D R T G M X
M N R Y L F T E O O Y I B W F
K E B L D H J L N N W S T O R
R W Y X D G P L I E A H Y L D
R D P T E R R I G T Y E T L R
B A J T A V J F H N K R R A L
R Y W B R N F R T T F E R F G
```

Allow me to wake

and all I hold dear

Bless me tonight

Filled with love

In every way

The day is done

The night is here

to a brand new day

Solution on page 60

The Myth of Cerridwen's Cauldron

Cerridwen was a wise Goddess whose magick was very powerful. She was often thought of as Queen of the Witches because She was so good at making magick brews, potions, and spells. She also had a cauldron that, when She stirred a potion inside, helped to make the brew even stronger.

Cerridwen had two sons; the oldest was named Morfran and the younger was called Gwion. Morfran felt that he was not as smart as most of the other children and this made him very sad. He would often come home crying and could not be consoled. He so loved all the beautiful trees, blue sky, flowers, and animals, and longed to write poetry in their honor—but he just didn't know enough words to do this. He could feel the words in his heart, but he wasn't smart enough to write as he wanted.

Because She loved Morfran very much, Cerridwen didn't like seeing Her son so upset and decided to help him. One bright Ostara (day of the Spring Equinox), She was picking herbs in her garden to use in a magick potion to make Morfran become the smartest boy in the world. She would make the potion in Her special cauldron and stir it for a year and a day so it would be as powerful as possible. As She picked the largest, most beautiful sunflowers and the greenest, strongest sage, She sang:

Sunflower, sunflower
yellow as the sun
bring Morfran wisdom
at a year plus one.
Let him be wise
Let him think
After this potion
he does drink.
Sage, sage,
bringer of smarts,
Help Morfran be
great at the arts.
Let him write,
Let him rhyme
After drinking this potion
in due time.

Over and over She sang these words, charging the newly-picked herbs with Her wishes. When Her basket was filled to the rim, She returned home and began making Her magick. Her large, black cauldron was already filled with rainwater, so Cerridwen simply added Her herbs, singing Her song all the while.

The powerful cauldron was so eager to please Cerridwen and do its job that it boiled, snapped and gurgled in tune with Her magickal song. The best thing with which to stir a large cauldron is a broomstick, so that is exactly what She did, chanting these words:

Broomstick, stir the potion well
Help My son be wise.
Potion I see, potion I smell
Hear My poor son's cries.

Once the potion was carefully put together, all it needed was to be stirred for a year and a day. Cerridwen's important work was done, so She thought She would finally take a break. Her youngest son, Gwion, passed by and She called to him:

Gwion, Gwion, come here to Me!
Stir the cauldron, three times three.
My work is done; I cannot stay...
Stir the cauldron a year and a day.

Gwion immediately obeyed his mother and began to stir the cauldron. Cerridwen was by now very hungry, so She decided to catch something for dinner. She shapeshifted into a lioness and went off to hunt deer.

As Gwion stirred the cauldron for an entire year, he saw all the seasons of the Wheel of the Year pass by. He saw the distant fires of Beltaine; he felt the heat of Midsummer...still Gwion stirred. He quietly remembered the god Lugh at Lughnassad and celebrated the autumn Equinox at Mabon...still Gwion stirred. He heard the spirits of Samhain, felt the chilly weather of the Yule season...still Gwion stirred. There was Imbolc in February and another Ostara in March...then Gwion's stirring got slower.

He knew that he had stirred for an entire year and that there was only one day left.

The next day, Gwion could tell that the magickal concoction was finally ready; the broomstick could barely move in the thickening potion and he had to stir as hard as he could. The liquid in the cauldron was still popping,

boiling, and gurgling in a regular rhythm. Gwion thought that he could almost hear words through the bubbles bursting on the potion's surface. He leaned his head closer to the potion, being careful not to be burned by the cauldron's fire. This was the chant he heard:

> I am the strongest, strongest brew
> Full of knowledge I'll give to you.
> One little drop is all it'll take—
> You'll have great knowledge when you wake.

With that, the potion came to a wild, rolling boil and—OUCH!—three drops of powerful brew popped onto Gwion's lips. Before he could even think, he licked his lips, tasting the potion, and instantly fell asleep.

By this time, Cerridwen was coming back to check on the potion and saw Gwion fast asleep. She knew that if one tasted it, the potion would make that one fall into a deep slumber—so Gwion must have stolen the magick intended for Morfran!

She was so angry at Gwion that She shrieked loudly, "Aaaaaah!" startling Gwion wide awake. He was so frightened by her screams that he began to run and shapeshifted into a rabbit. Cerridwen took off after him and shapeshifted into a cougar, catching up to Gwion very quickly. Just before She reached him, Gwion used his new brain and again 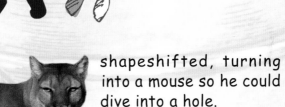 shapeshifted, turning into a mouse so he could dive into a hole.

But, his mother was too fast for him. She shapeshifted into an owl and swooped down from the sky!

Thinking quickly, Gwion turned himself into a turtle and Cerridwen could not get her owl's beak around his shell, but She still attacked and pecked at him. Thinking he could hide in the tall weeds, Gwion turned himself into a kernel of corn. Cerridwen then shapeshifted into a chicken and ate him up!

The kernel of corn, now in Her stomach, was full of magickal knowledge. Cerridwen's stomach got larger and larger with the growing kernel of corn. Nine months later, She gave birth to a son who was, indeed, the same child as Gwion, since he'd grown from the same kernel of corn. She was still angry, but the child was so beautiful that She could not kill him. Instead, she put him in a basket and left him in the woods.

The same day, a king's son was taking a stroll in the quiet woods and happened upon Gwion. The man was so taken by the child's sparkling beauty that he could not take his eyes off the baby. As he stared into the basket, the king's son said, "I shall name him Taliesin, as it is the nicest name I know and it befits a baby of his remarkable beauty. I will take him home to raise as my own son."

Since the baby still had the magick of Cerridwen's potion, Taliesin grew up to be the greatest poet in all of Wales.

*** **Short explanation of the myth:** As all myths, the story of Cerridwen's cauldron is meant to teach us. Her cauldron stands for rebirth, in that whoever drinks the magick potion will be transformed. Also, the idea of shapeshifting stands for change, or transformation. As the cauldron is stirred throughout the seasons of the Wheel of the Year, much change is shown. At the end of the story, Cerridwen was going to kill Gwion, but doesn't (shows change of heart).

Simply put, this story was meant to tell us that change and rebirth are under the control of Cerridwen, a very powerful Celtic goddess.

Side Note: Traditionally, in Wicca, the cauldron (especially with shimmery water inside) is symbolic of the moon and of the Goddess.

The Cauldron of Cerridwen

Find the words in the grid. Words can go horizontally, vertically and diagonally in all eight directions.

```
S P O R D E E R H T K Z R C
K X B V C N A R F R O M E M
E S H A P E S H I F T R W P
R K Q X R S C A U L D R O N
N N Q Z B V M T R C L F L K
E O G L F R E A E Q D T F M
L W I P N O O R R M R T N Z
O L G W P J R O E T A T U V
F E K T G I R G M L X R S V
C D L K D T A X E S H H B T
O G T W H S C I R W T W M C
R E E C N N S K I Z F I N T
N N P W K I V G T F J F C C
L K K L N L H X S X L X Y K
```

broomstick
cauldron
Cerridwen
Gwion
kernel of corn
knowledge
Morfran
poet
sage
shapeshift
smart
stir

sunflower
Taleisin
three drops

Solution on page 61

Wheel of the Year

Most of us have seen a calendar. A calendar shows us the days of the week, the months of the year, and often shows us the dates of certain holidays. Pagans use a Wheel of the Year to show the changing of the seasons and our holidays or Sabbats.

We think of the wheel constantly turning with the seasons. The Wheel of the Year is used to divide the year into seasons and celebrations of our religion. In this book is a picture of how you should think of the Wheel of the Year. First, I will name the Greater and Lesser Sabbats; later I will explain what each day means to us.

The Wheel of the Year looks like a huge circle, which is thought of as the entire year. The circle is then divided into sections representing seasons. We have what is known as the Eight Sabbats, or celebrations. We have Lesser Sabbats, known as Quarters and we have Greater Sabbats, which are also known as Cross-Quarters. Lesser Sabbats are the solstices and equinoxes of the year and there are four:

- Yule (Winter Solstice), which occurs on or about December 21;
- Ostara (Spring Equinox), which falls on or about March 21;
- Midsummer or Litha (Summer Solstice) around June 21; and
- Mabon (Fall/Autumn Equinox) about Sept 21.

There are also four Greater Sabbats, or Cross-Quarters:

- Samhain on October 31,
- Imbolc on February 2,
- Beltaine on May 1, and
- Lammas or Lughnassad (depending on your tradition) on August 1.

Now we can discuss what each celebration means to us.

37

(October 31) Samhain

(October 31) Samhain, a Greater Sabbat, is the Wiccan New Year. This is when we honor and remember our ancestors who have crossed the veil (those who have passed away). We believe that the veil between the worlds of the living and the dead is at its thinnest at this time of year, so that it allows us to more easily honor and send messages to our family members or loved ones who have passed. We also try to let go of bad habits, being upset or angry, and any other things that can cause harm. Many people of other religions have now loosely adopted the customs of the Pagan Sabbat of Samhain and call it Halloween.

(December 21) Yule

(December 21) Yule, a Lesser Sabbat, is also known as Winter Solstice. This is when we celebrate the sun's return, after a long winter has been endured. Although winter is not over, we see this as the beginning of longer days and more daylight. Many traditions see this as the birth of the young God.

(February 2) Imbolc

(February 2) Imbolc, also known as Candlemas, is a Greater Sabbat honoring the Goddess Brighid (also known as Brigit or Brid,) who is a very important Goddess to the Celtic traditions. She is patron goddess of healing and of bounty and fertility. She is also known as a Goddess of Light.

(March 21) Ostara

(March 21) Ostara, a Lesser Sabbat, is also known as Spring Equinox. As Pagans, this is when we celebrate the coming of Spring. This celebration is named after the Greek Goddess Oester. Ostara has been adopted by other religions as Easter which is celebrated at around the same time.

(April 30 or May 1) Beltaine

(April 30 or May 1) Beltaine is a Greater Sabbat at which we celebrate the young God Bel. The word "Beltaine" originally meant "Bel-Fire," and since this is one of the Fire Festivals, balefires are usually lit at this time of year. Celtic traditions often see Beltaine and Samhain as the most important celebrations.

Wheel of the Year

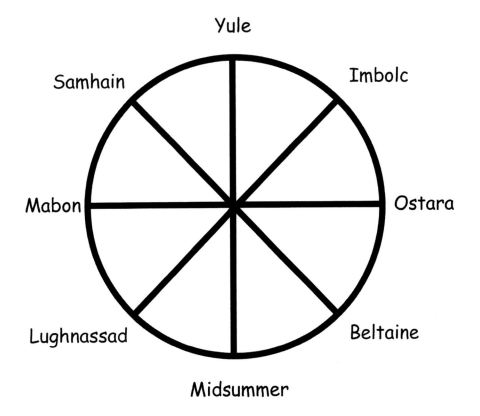

Yule

Imbolc

Samhain

Ostara

Mabon

Beltaine

Lughnassad

Midsummer

Practice Drawing the Wheel of the Year Below:

Wheel of the Year

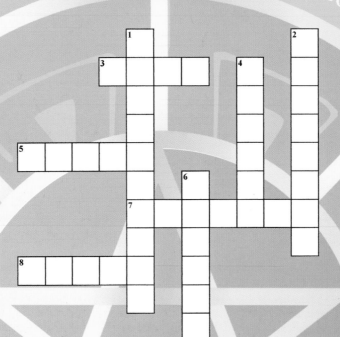

(c) Raine Hill

ACROSS

3 Lesser Sabbat also known as Winter Solstice; the return of the Sun God who is borne of the Goddess.

5 Lesser Sabbat marking the Autumn Equinox; we should give thanksgiving for the fruits of the Earth.

7 Greater Sabbat celebrated in October to honor our ancestors; marks the last harvest; this is the night that the veil is at its thinnest.

8 Lesser Sabbat also known as Summer Solstice.

DOWN

1 Greater Sabbat; Marks first harvest of the year and the God's symbolic "death".

2 Greater Sabbat; Fire festival marking the beginning of summer season.

4 Lesser Sabbat celebrating the midpoint of Spring, where light and day achieve perfect balance. Light will now be on the increase.

6 Greater Sabbat celebrated in February that honors the Goddess Brighid.

Eight Sabbats

Find the words in the grid. Words can go horizontally, vertically and diagonally in all eight directions.

```
W R B B T H I R D H A R V E S T K
T G H K C H D G G L F F M Y R V N
N D A R K M Y S T E R I E S V G B
Y N K W L E C R H R H D H B R G R
F D U J Q M N R H J M P P E B A N
I N R N L V L D H T B W A Q E F K
R A T D D C B P O X R T B Y B N D
E L R F F E J C J F E I W L T V S
F R L V D W R X K R S E B K M G R
E E Z V H K K W S X N U C E P C O
S M Z W R R L A O C J R M T R F T
T M G W T K B M I R Q C G M P X S
I U D R E B O T C O L Q X B E M E
V S V N A P L G T X V D Z D L R C
A B T T H E F K B L K V F F K W N
L L G H C Y F Z K M K L R T V T A
V E I L A T I T S T H I N N E S T
```

© 2008 Raine Hill.

Ancestors

Celtic New Year

Dark Mysteries

End of Summer

Fire Festival

Greater Sabbat

October

Rebirth

Summerland

Third Harvest

Underworld

Veil at its Thinnest

Solution on page 62

The Spiral and Triskele

The spiral may be the oldest symbol of any religion. It has been found drawn on large rocks and cave walls of ancient peoples from many, many years ago. In Ireland, there is the ancient Burial Chamber of Newgrange that is more than 5,000 years old. At the entrance, there is a large rock with spirals carved all over it. It seems that the spiral was very important to these ancient people so very long ago. What the spiral meant to them is unknown, but we can guess that it stands for the path that they saw the sun make across the sky as the months went by.

When you go inside the hallways of the cave, you can see a triple spiral, or triskele, carved on the wall. Inside the burial chamber, the roof is open so that the sun shines directly onto the burial site at a precise moment on the Winter Solstice. The Newgrange chamber is a very sacred place where many people visit each year.

Many people of Pagan and Wiccan traditions also feel that the spiral has deep meaning. We look at it as being a symbol of the triple Goddess: Maiden, Mother and Crone. Some use the spiral, or the triskele, as a symbol for the Celtic Goddess Brighid. Others may see the triple spiral as a symbol of the seasons "dying" and being "reborn" as they do each year.

On the following page you can practice drawing the Spiral and the Triskele.

Spiral

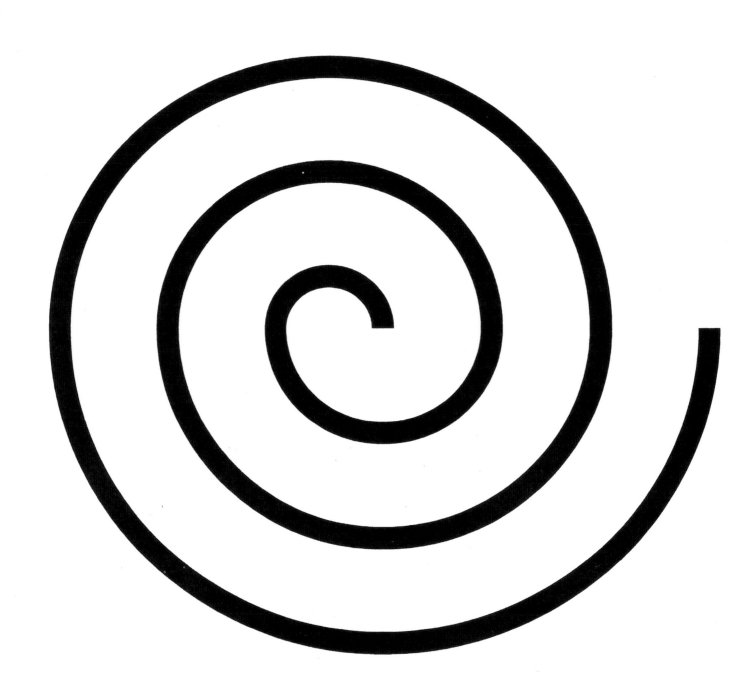

Practice Drawing the Spiral Here:

Triskele

Practice Drawing the Triskele Here:

The Pentacle is a Sacred Symbol

Probably the most important symbol to Wiccans is the pentacle. A pentacle is a five-pointed star (usually with one point upright) encased in a circle. This is a sacred symbol to Pagans. Most of us wear a pentacle on a chain or cord as a necklace. It reminds us that we are being protected by the Higher Powers and it is a symbol of our religion.

The circle around the five-pointed star symbolizes the sacred circle, or protected place, that Witches use for worship and ritual. The points of a pentacle each stand for an element. In many traditions the topmost point stands for our Spirit, the top right point stands for the element of Water, the bottom right stands for Fire. The top left point stands for the element of Air and the bottom left point symbolizes the element of Earth. Many Witches display a pentacle on our altars and use it in many rituals, as we believe it to be a symbol of great power and strength. Study the pentacle and its elements on the next page. Learn where each element is on the pentacle.

Pentacle

Spirit

Air

Water

Earth

Fire

Practice Drawing the Pentacle with Elements Below:

Solution on page 63

Final Assessment

Instructions

Before you write in your name on the Certificate of Achievement, you must pass this assessment of what you have learned. If you miss more than two questions, you'll need to go back and take a look at the topics where you had difficulties; and then try the assessment again! (You will earn five points for each question you answer correctly.) If you don't pass the first time, don't worry. Have fun with the book again and again until you can answer the questions correctly. We all have to learn before we can fly! In this assessment you will find:

1. True or false questions. Circle either "T" for true or "F" for false.
2. Multiple choice questions. Circle the correct answer.
3. Essay questions. You will need to write your answers in the area provided.

Good Luck!

True or False?

1. T or F
Ostara is a sabbat that honors the Goddess Macha.

2. T or F
There are twelve sabbats on the Wheel of the Year.

3. T or F
The sabbat of Lughnassad is also known as Lammas.

4. T or F
Imbolc is in the month of December.

5. T or F
Samhain is the Wiccan New Year.

6. T or F
The pentacle looks like a triple spiral, an ancient symbol.

7. T or F
When the moon is waxing, it looks as if it is getting bigger in the sky.

Multiple Choice

8. The color associated with the West is _____?

Green
Yellow
Blue

9. This Lesser Sabbat is also known as Winter Solstice.

Yule
Samhain
Imbolc

10. The Element of the North is _____?

Earth
Air
Fire

11. The Four Directions are also called _____?

Halves
Quarters
Pennies

12. The Element of the South is _____?

Water
Earth
Fire

13. The topmost point of the upright pentacle stands for _____.

Fire
Air
Spirit

14. The _____ is a triple spiral, an ancient symbol.

pentacle
triskele
cauldron

Essay Questions

15. I know the short version of the Wiccan Rede as taught in this book!
(Write the rede in the space below)

_____

_____

_____

_____

_____

_____

_____

_____

16. I know the Morning Blessing! (Write the blessing in the space below)

_____

_____

_____

_____

17. I know the Nighttime Blessing! (Write the blessing in the space below)

_____

_____

_____

_____

_____

_____

_____

_____

18. I can name the Eight Pagan Sabbats!

1. _____

2. _____

3. _____

4. _____

5. _____

6. _____

7. _____

8. _____

19. I can name the Elements of the five points of the Pentacle!

1. _____

2. _____

3. _____

4. _____

5. _____

20. I have made an altar of my very own. This is what I have on it so far:

_____

_____

_____

_____

I am proud to award this

Certificate of Achievement

To

Great Job

_____

For earning an outstanding

Score on the Final Test of

Growing Up Pagan: A Workbook for Pagan Families

Raine Hill

Answer Keys

The First Battle of the Gods and the Giants
A Creation Story

Solution:

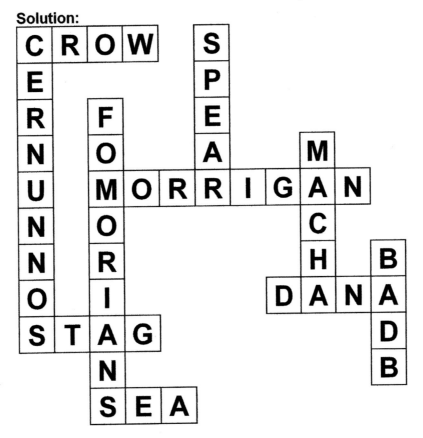

The First Battle of the Gods and the Giants

Pandora's Box Crossword

Solution:

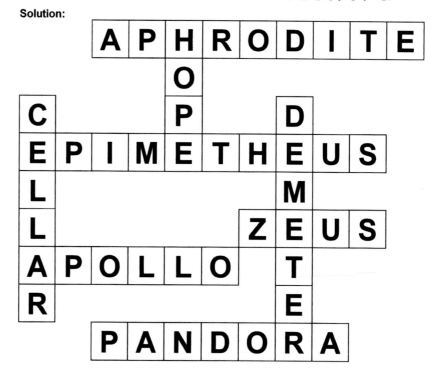

The Myth of Pandora's Box

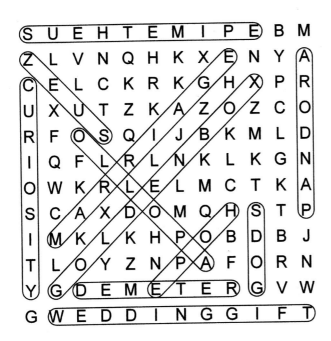

The Four Quarters

Solution:

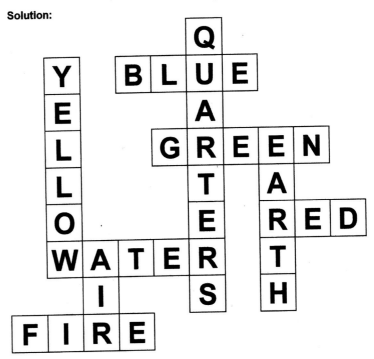

Morning Blessing

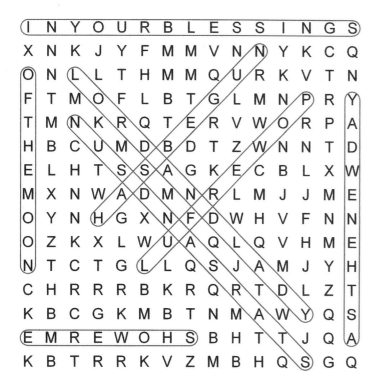

```
I N Y O U R B L E S S I N G S
X N K J Y F M M V N N Y K C Q
O N L L T H M M Q U R K V T N
F T M O F L B T G L M N P R Y
T M N K R Q T E R V W O R P A
H B C U M D B D T Z W N N T D
E L H T S S A G K E C B L X W
M X N W A D M N R L M J M E
O Y N H G X N F D W H V F N N
O Z K X L W U A Q L Q V H M E
N T C T G L L Q S J A M J Y H
C H R R R B K R R T D L Z T S
K B C G K M B T N M A W Y Q A
E M R E W O H S B H T T J Q A
K B T R R K V Z M B H Q S G Q
```

Nighttime Blessing

```
N T N W A X P E N T M Z H K F
K T N N N J L V B H B T H E G
P O G M A B T O L E E M T H N
P A C L A R B L S D I N L D J
M B F W L B L H S A N H L A N
C R R C L V L T M Y E I J J D
V A R X I R B I S V G N J J V
Z N K D H F K W E R G T H T
M D M R O M C D T D N I G B T
M N R Y L F T E O O E H T B
K E B L D H J L T N R I B T W
R W Y X D G P L I E A H Y T D
R D P T E R R I T W S Y T A D
B A J T A V J F H N K R R A L
R Y W B R N F R T T T F E R F G
```

The Cauldron of Cerridwen

```
S P O R D E E R H T  K Z  R  C
K X B V C N A R F R O M  E  M
E S H A P E S H I F T  R  W  P
R K Q X R S C A U L D R O  N
N N Q Z B V M T R C L F  L  K
E O G L F R E A E Q D T  F  M
L W I P N O O R R M R T  N  Z
O L G W P J R O E T A T  U  V
F E K T G I R G M L X R  S  V
C D L K D T A X E S H H  B  T
O G T W H S C I R W T W  M  C
R E E C N N S K I Z F I  N  T
N N P W K I V G T F J F  C  C
  L K K L N L H X S X L  X  Y K
```

Wheel of the Year

Solution:

Eight Sabbats

Answer Key for Final Assessment

True or False

1. F
2. F
3. T
4. F
5. T
6. F
7. T

Multiple Choice

8. Blue
9. Yule
10. Earth
11. Quarters
12. Fire
13. Spirit
14. Triskele

Essay Questions

15.
Bide the Wiccan Law ye Must
In Perfect Love and Perfect Trust.
Eight Words the Wiccan Rede Fulfill:
'An ye Harm None, Do as ye Will.
What ye put Forth will Come Back to Thee
So ever Mind the Law of Three.
Follow This in Mind and Heart;
Merry ye Meet and Merry ye Part.

16.
Powerful Lord and Lady
of the moon, stars and sun
Shower me in Your blessings
as the new day has begun.

17.
The day is done
The night is here
Bless me tonight
And all I hold dear.
Allow me to wake
To a brand new day
Filled with love
In every way.

18.
1. Samhain
2. Yule (or Winter Solstice)
3. Imbolc
4. Ostara (or Spring Equinox)
5. Beltaine
6. Litha (or Midsummer or Summer Solstice)
7. Lughnassad (or Lammas)
8. Mabon (or Fall Equinox)

19.
1. Spirit
2. Water
3. Fire
4. Air
5. Earth

20. If you have made an altar of your own, you've earned five points!